THE BRAND *BESIDE* THE BRAND

10 Reasons to step from behind

and stand beside the brand

By LaRita Shelby ©2016

Published by SB Media

A division of SB Music, Media & Marketing

& Shall Be Productions

Sherman Oaks, California

The Brand Beside The Brand

**10 Reasons to step from behind
and stand beside the brand**

By LaRita Shelby ©2016

Published by SB Media

13547 Ventura Blvd. #678 Sherman Oaks, CA 91423

www.LaRitaShelby.com

Cover design by Prophecy Web Designs

Cover photo by BK Thomas

Images in the book are license free under

Creative Commons from Pexels.com

All rights reserved. No part of this book may be used or re-produced in any form without permission from the author or representative of SB Media.

ISBN 10   09712021-9-2

ISBN 13   978-0-9712021-9-1

Library of Congress Control Number 2016915151

SAN 253-9551

Acknowledgements

To my late Aunt Mary, whom I often quote and who said; "Nothing beats failure but a try." Her effervescent spirit and potent words of wisdom carry me from day to day and from challenge to victory every time. I would like to thank my family and extended family that remain. Claudia, Dorie, Andrea, my son Justin, Eddie, Rod, Dank, Stan, Sterling, Ray, Mike, Marquelyn, David, Martin & Markus. To Cerise & Elvin, Felicia, Joyce, Janet, Carlton, Dr. Clanton, Carl & Christine Johnson, Delia, George Barnes, Levi & Debbie Frazier, Karen Moore, Queen Ruby Wilson, Debra Smith, The Millers, Fords, Greens & Davenports, Sterling Jr., Tony, Jackie Jr., Marcia, Muggie, Muriel, Nikki, Kim, Alexia, Brad & Joan Sanders, Dr. Ariedelle Shelby Stewart, Dr. James Stewart, William & Annie Mount, Irene Shelby Ward, Walter Shelby, Joe & Dorothy Shelby, Benny & Calvin Shelby, Wendy Moten, Willie Martin, Vida Nash and Dr. Farah Gray.

To Lee Bailey, Tom Joyner, Jerome V. Carter, poet & genius Roni Walter, 1 Plus One Management Inc., Prophecy Productions, Attorney Venus Griffith, Gail Gibson, Denise Pines, Dr. Daphne Bolden, my BFF in the U.K. Joy Montgomery and to Janet, D'Angela, Marcella and T'Keyah. To May May Ali and T'Keyah Crystal Keyman, thank you. To Sandra Evers-Manly, John Forbes & BHERC thank you.

Special thanks to Michael Tushman, Chair of Leadership Development at Harvard Business School and Charles A. O'Reilly, Frank E. Buck Professor of Management at the Graduate School of Business at Stanford University.

I would also like to thank Linda Ackerman Anderson and Dean Anderson, authors of Beyond Change Management and The Change Leader's Roadmap. Also thanks to Northrop Grumman, Jazz Preservationist Linda Morgan, Latwania Neasman, Oscar Generale, King of Product Placement for the Cannes Film Festival, Barbara Lindsey, Yolanda Bozant, Greg and Andrea Southern of LMS Wings Corporation, Attorney and author Roderick K. Porter, Media Artists Group, Troy Tieuel of the Los Angeles Sentinel, Anna Fuson of Red Sea Entertainment, Dr. Logan H. Westbrooks of Ascent Publishing, Prophecy Web Designs and to Dr. Karen Savlov of Touro University.

To the many media professionals that I have encountered along the way and to the schools and businesses who put your faith in me, I thank you one and all.

Note from the author

After years of acquiring millionaire friends who sought my advice, it dawned upon me that one of the things I was helping them to do was to shape the personal entity that was associated with their products or services, as well as give guidance about marketing and promoting their business.

One of the people who inspired me to write this book became a millionaire at a very young age and though he had amassed great wealth, he was inexperienced at buying media for TV and radio. He had other staff members but trusted my advice about how to get the most out of his marketing budget. When we met I was someone who stood behind the brand that I worked for. The young millionaire met me in the capacity of journalist and producer for a radio program and an online publication. My friend had no idea that I had any marketing savvy but we kept in touch. After several conversations, he realized that I had strengths outside of the capacity that we had originally met.

I admit that I was not always sure how to present myself as a multi-faceted businessperson. I had free range to do so because I was an independent contractor, not an employee who was bound by any restrictions. I had a fear of how I might be perceived by others if I laid it down on the line as far as all of the things that I could do. While I do promote a focused and concise business effort and ethic, I had some personal growth to do and it took courage to come to the conclusion of where I am now. I share many reasons for making a change and ten steps to show you how. In this book I hope that you will find great value. Here's to your success.

Contents

Step 1	Just BE: Boldly Exist	11
Step 2	You are the brand	25
Step 3	Revise your networking psyche	34
Step 4	Arrive more quickly at your decisions	39
Step 5	Support outward decisions	42
Step 6	Devise a strategy	46
Step 7	Insist on brand name identity	61
Step 8	Insist on your value	76
Step 9	Commit to expanding your turf	89
Step 10	Reflect, inspect and project	98
Bonus:	Dealing with difficult people	110
	Being The Brand Beside The Brand	127

Step One: Just B.E. Boldly Exist!

Doing comes out of being and being comes out of knowing your story. What's yours? Here is a little bit of mine.

Life has now given me every reason to just be, to **boldly exist** and to be unapologetically and unequivocally me. When I published my first two books, I adopted another radical theory that helped me to cross the finish line. In those cases, I had to abandon perfection and embrace completion. For years I had waited for the perfect set of circumstances to get my product out there. I had met a dynamo (Denise Pines) early in her career and she had just published Tavis Smiley's first book entitled Just A Thought.

She liked my idea for a little book of quotes consisting of catchy one liners that would be marketed to women who love to go shopping. It was never meant to be a literary benchmark, just a pocket sized humorous conversation piece that we would sell for about ten dollars. Pines One Publishing was off and running. Smiley's book was her first and my book was to be her second. Well we all know what happened. Tavis Smiley's career took off like a rocket and she helped him build a multi-media empire. The Smiley brand grew from Denise's early publishing efforts to bestselling partnerships with Doubleday, Atrium, Hay House and more. The TV brand grew also to include enormously profitable ventures with PBS, NPR, Public Radio International, CSPAN, Microsoft and more. I was in for a long wait for Denise to have the time to commit to my little humorous book and so the project sat for many years. I did not have the team in place to move forward without them, or so I thought.

A few years later I had amassed several writings of plays, poetry and prose. Some of the pieces had been performed in ensemble presentations, and after each event I was approached by someone who was surprised by my writing ability. One night after a stage presentation of a work titled "Feelings" presented by Nikki Johnson and Associates, two very well-known writers and producers approached me separately. One was Michael Ajakwe and the other was Sy Richardson, also a respected director. "Feelings" contained several of my writings and both Sy and Michael encouraged me to go further. At the time I was quite comfortable financially, I juggled multiple radio contracts, and I frequently worked in TV and film. I heard them but had no need to write except to 'free my soul'—translation: to get whatever was on my mind off of it and on to the page. In other words, the marketplace was different then. The environment that supported my lifestyle was set to a different pulse back then. The process by which I sought work and quickly acquired it was different.

For seven years I was a contractor with the Department of Defense and provided radio entertainment via my self-titled show for Armed Forces Television and Radio Services. The time commitment for that one contract was usually limited to one or two days per week. During the rest of the time I was making money in other fun and fulfilling ways. I had contracts on two nationally syndicated radio shows, Lee Bailey's RadioScope and The Tom Joyner Morning Show. With those contracts, plus my work in TV and film, I was somewhere around the six figure salary mark every year. I had not hit my million yet, but I was comfortable.

In 1997 things started to change, one by one my radio contracts ended. Reality TV and the labor union environment in Los Angeles was greatly downsizing the amount of scripted television shows and film productions that were based in California. I was about to enter a long dry season. I had proudly *stood behind* major brands like Armed Forces Radio, Lee Bailey's RadioScope and the Tom Joyner Morning Show, which had eight million listeners.

Most of Mr. Joyner's fans had no idea that I was the voice of two of their favorite characters on the It's Your World Radio drama that aired twice daily. On any given day you could have heard me in 57 countries over the Armed Forces Network worldwide, I was an announcer on RadioScope, which was on in 150 markets in the U. S. and the short form version of the urban entertainment program was aired in my show internationally, as well as On The Phone With TiRone (another popular syndicated segment that aired stateside).

In standing behind the brands, enjoying the work and just looking forward to the paycheck, I missed an opportunity to re-position myself in a manner that could have attracted other high caliber work to me, instead of me being on the chase for it. Sadly, by the time I realized that this is what I should have done, the moment was gone.

Where are you right now as a business, a professional, a personality or an entrepreneur? Where are you headed? Whether it's raw ambition, a shifting economy or changes in lifestyle, if you are contemplating why you should move forward and how, the book outlines the reasons and methods you can use now to re-position yourself as a brand.

I became motivated to write because now I see my writing not only as a means of expression but finally, as a product and a new revenue stream. I have vowed to wait no more. My first two books were self-published several years ago. I rushed to get the books done in time to market them at a major festival. They are imperfect and modest in quality but I got over the fear of being imperfect, the fear of being judged and the fear of a new process. It became imperative that I do things differently because the world that I once knew has changed and it will never be exactly the same again.

When the global economy thrives all industries are impacted positively. When there is a decline it is also felt worldwide. If for any reason you (or your company) are currently in transition, think of the reasons why. There are only two reasons for the need for change. Either something happened that was totally out of your control or something happened that was within your control, but you did not prevent it or see it coming. Either way here you are, and yes things have drastically changed in the marketplace. Let's take a look.

According to Bureau of Labor Statistics, at the time of publication, the number of persons employed part time for economic reasons was at about 6.0 million. These people are also referred to as involuntary part time workers who would have preferred full time work but their hours were cut or they could only find part time work. (Bureau of Labor May 6, 2016) The unemployment rate had dropped to 5.9%; which still accounted for 7.9 million unemployed.

It is a sobering fact that a record number of people will always still be looking for work. Many households will experience compromised levels of disposable income. That means that if you're in business, or work for a business, there will be more competition to gain customers for whatever it is that you are selling. There will be more people who are fighting for the same dollars, the same contracts, the same opportunities. This may be no great revelation, but in light of this we all have to seize every opportunity to be outstanding, think outside the box, and discover ways to make the most unique pitch and sincere presentation possible to accurately represent who you are and what you do. That includes presenting yourself in a renewed idea of branding. You must boldly exist.

If you have already grasped a bold approach when it comes to presenting yourself, then congratulations. If you are still passive, shy or uncertain, I am not suggesting that you adapt an arrogant or pretentious posture as you approach potential clients, business partners or customers. The statement about being bold, means that your confidence factor (or your employees' confidence factor) must be in peak performance. You must be the brand beside the brand.

1 A) Advertise the product and promote the story.

The best way to exude confidence is to advertise the product, and promote the story. You may ask, how do I do this? A personal touch has always made a compelling difference in consumer relations and this is how your story stands beside the brand. The product has its own attributes, and you can recite those from your head, or what is known as your cognitive faculties. Promoting "the story" refers to what you have personally witnessed about how this product has changed lives, or how having an opportunity to work with this product, company or project has changed your life. Promoting the story may also include how you hope that it will impact your life or the lives of others. This "story" is generated from your personality or your emotional center. An important note here is to really be authentic. Usually people can detect an ostentatious demeanor. I liken it to the telemarketers who make sales calls and though they attempt to sound genuine, you can always tell that they are reading from a script, and that there is nothing personal or sincere about their encounter with you. Most of us have a very low tolerance for such, and even folks who are rather nice during the day, quickly become agitated and abruptly end the call with little or no adherence to what the caller is saying, selling or intending.

If telling your own story is not appropriate or applicable to your product or business, then if you probe deeply enough there is usually a story elsewhere. Quite often it's a transformational story, about how the company was founded, or by whom. It may be a story of how someone overcame adversity or has sought to improve some facet of life. I'm suggesting that the story has value, and your value is increased when you can zero in on this story and couple it with how you approach the marketplace. While working as Director of Digital Strategy for the online publishing platform (www.EURweb.com) we were approached by a company that specialized in blue jeans and denim wear for curvy women. It was the holiday season and they wanted to run an ad campaign. After careful consultation with them, we devised a strategy to not only run their ads but to expand the reach of the ads by creating a series that personalized what it meant for women as well as men, when they experience a great pair of jeans that fit. The series was called "I Am Entitled." It originated on our site, it engaged the audience and was cross promoted on social media, and it went viral! "I Am Entitled" became the voice of the brand, while the great art and graphics of the ad embodied the image of the brand. The story was that everyone was happy when they found a great pair of fitting jeans.

The 21st century started with great anticipation, but before the first decade was done, we saw a plunge in the global economy. Between 2007 and 2008 world news reported a global financial crisis, which was said to have been the worst since the great depression of the 1930's. The stock market plunged, the housing market tanked and many financial institutions faced utter calamity due to the influx of subprime lending. Once the housing bubble burst, the fallout continued downhill, ultimately impacting major banks in the U. S. and the auto industry. Some auto companies and banks received assistance from the federal government. These were bail outs, and depending upon political views they either were a sign of salvation or poorly advised actions that spelled more of an economic downfall.

Indeed, things changed and if you have heard of the book Who Moved My Cheese by Dr. Spencer Johnson

(G. P. Putnam's Sons Publishing 1998), well yes- someone moved your cheese, and if you're like me, they ate it!

Cheese is a metaphor for when change has happened and the challenge is to either lament the obstacles that the change has created or accept the change. One also has the option of quickly adapting and preparing for the opportunities that the change has now presented. With a permanent shift in the job market and the global economy, it is safe to say that it is imperative that we look at all things differently.

Many companies and individuals have rebounded. Yet the pressure is on to be more competitive, to do things faster, better and at a more efficient cost or to scale your business so that it is attractive to more customers. Still within the gap there is the issue of brand awareness and market competition.

Here are some questions that may arise. How can I maximize my reach? What incentives are there for me or my company? Can I barter and trade goods or services? How can I generate press and public relations for me as an employee, or as a corporation or small business owner? How can I manage the image that my customers or employees can instantly transmit on social media?

This book provides steps to help you create a new vision for going forward. Be bold about accepting the changes that have brought you to this point. If the corporate giants of the world have had to regroup, then from this point on let's boldly accept that this is true for you too and declare to boldly exist in all that you do! Just BE!

Step Two: You are the brand!

Given the facts in chapter one, hopefully you can agree that you absolutely cannot look at things in the same way. It is time to fully embrace a new vision, you are the brand. Yes, you should recognize that you are just as important as the product or service itself. I'd like to offer a juxtaposition here that suggests that you shift your thinking from seeing your product, goods or services as something that exists outside of yourself, to seeing those same products, goods or services as being an extension of yourself. This is a significant shift in thinking whether you are an employee, a contractor or a business owner. There is an old notion that a company stands behind their products. They back whatever it is that they are making or selling. Employees or contractors assumed this same mindset. That was fine when one could expect to hire good workers and incubate them for 20 or 30 years, retiring them with a compensation plan that they could live off of for the rest of their years. As an employee, you could afford to stand behind a company because the company stood behind you. While this ideal segue and long term engagement may exist for some percentage of the work force, nowadays the tenure for employees is much shorter. In most cases, there are more free agents, home based businesses and independent contractors in the marketplace. Your stake in whatever company you own, work for, contract or represent is much higher. Therefore, you must re-evaluate your self-importance and how it relates to the brand itself. Let's test this with a routine analysis.

Do you ever go into a store and need assistance? It doesn't matter what kind of store or type of assistance you need. What matters is that you find someone with whom you identify as a part of that company. As soon as you see someone with a logo on their shirt or even a name tag, they immediately become The Brand, the store, the person upon which the store's entire reputation rests. The store that has lured you in may have been in business for decades, and may have spent millions of dollars in advertising. It also doesn't matter if you came to the store to buy a pack of nails, a lawnmower or an entire kitchen set, the person that you meet at the point of contact becomes the brand. The same brand value is now assigned to you, right here, right now no matter what stage of your career you are experiencing. If you haven't adopted this mindset, then the time to do so is now. Many conscientious corporations already regard everyone in the organization as valued team members. But do you really wholeheartedly see yourself as such? If so, then think of yourself as having received a hefty raise in your mental valuation. By embracing this mindset, you should act as if there is a major promotion that is going to happen at your company and it's already been narrowed down to you and one other person. A shift in mindset is the beginning of a shift in reality. If you diminish your value in your mind, it will appear in your actions, and it will show in how you regard all that matters to the business.

According to Dean Anderson and Linda Ackerman Anderson: "A critical mass of organization must operate from a new mindset and behavior for transformation to succeed and for new business models or direction to be sustained" (Ackerman-Anderson & Anderson, 2010, p. 53).

If you would rather stand behind your products and stay in the background, I send you best wishes for your success. I even commend you if your business is prosperous and you are able to do this. I would like to read your book someday, seriously I would. But from my analysis most businesses are in a race to keep up with the changing trends in technology. They are seeking all avenues to engage their customers more and more as an extension of their traditional advertising methods. Remember when you first heard about Facebook and Twitter? How many of you brushed it off as a fad? I know I did. How many of you also watched one major corporation after another leap into the atmosphere that is now known and valued as Social Media? A few years later Facebook's market value (at press time) was estimated in excess of $355 billion and Twitter was valued at around $10 billion. Other sites that are viable are

Pinterest (estimated value is $11 billion) Snapchat ($16 billion estimated value) Instagram and Vine.com (J. Hempel/Wired.com Feb 8, 2016). The actual numbers will vary as time goes on but the point here is to illuminate the fact that at one time these companies were unheard of. They were mere ideas held by someone who embodied a courageous vision while they worked for someone else's company or while they studied someone else's success and ideas before taking the leap and/or partnering with someone to bring their own vision to life. With that in mind, now think of yourself as a brand whose value has yet to be seen or realized for it's true worth.

You are to be commended for whatever has brought you to this moment in time. What have you done so far that has worked out every single time? I mean really think about it. Make a short list. You may have had a certain job description or you may have handled overlapping duties in the past with little or no single recognition for the duality of roles that you had to play in the success of your business or company that employed you. But what have you proven to be an expert at doing no matter what? Which brings me to the question.

What great assets can you take with you on your journey to be the brand beside the brand?

1. _____
2. _____
3. _____
4. _____
5. _____

Okay, from the list above, if you have answered honestly and not just from emotion, you have identified the things that you absolutely must take with you into your new phase. Now think about what you can add to this experience. What innovation must you embrace to be competitive? Has there been a theoretical or technological shift in the way that any of the skills above can be applied? Has there been any government deregulation or shift in the marketplace warranting the need for and application of these skills? If so, have you entertained how you can use these skills and remain competitive? Here's another quiz for you.

How would you fill in the blanks below? I know I'm good at what I have listed above, but it would help if I took a class or had additional training in:

1._____

2._____

3._____

Thank you for your honesty above. Now let's get brutally honest here. Of all of the great things that have brought you to this point, what are some things that have hindered you from making the progress you desire and know that is possible for you to achieve? I'll throw out a few examples, and as the saying goes, I may 'resemble a few of these remarks.' Do you trust people before they have proven themselves worthy of your time, talent or your business? For years I put myself and my business in vulnerable situations by trusting that I was dealing with people who I could take at their word. I am a city girl on the outside and a Southern girl at heart, and I was raised to keep my word. I was also encouraged not to give my word, if I could not keep my word. My Aunt Mary's famous saying was: "Think twice and speak once." I have lost thousands of dollars and even a triple A credit rating by entering into agreements with people who promised to pay for their part of an obligation or claimed that they were in a position to guarantee a contract award, only to find out that they were just talking and we all know what they say about talk... it's just cheap. Well cheap to them maybe, but the lesson is expensive when business matters are on the line.

Question: What must you leave behind?

1. _____
2. _____
3. _____

What are some other things to consider leaving behind? Do you procrastinate? Do you take on more than you can deliver? Do you constantly make concessions on your pricing for people who can afford to pay you more? Do you tell your dreams to the wrong people? Are you in partnership (personally or professionally) with people who share your vision? Are you allowing your emotions or a faith based mentality to override making a firm business decision? Does guilt, family ties or naivety interfere with your financial affairs? You can take it from here. Just really take a long, deep moment to think about this.

Moving forward, it is imperative that you show up as your *best **self*** to convince that customer, corporation, bank or organization that **who you are** and what you represent is a valuable investment.

Step Three: Revise your networking psyche to 25/5

If you have been to business and networking events, they pretty much start the same way. There is early morning coffee, an evening cocktail party, or perhaps a crowded convention floor. We vow to meet as many people as possible and leave with a stack of business cards or newly input contacts on our mobile devise. Some of us follow up with each person right away, but usually after a few months those business cards are added to a stack or the contacts fade further down the list, with a few exceptions.

Though our intentions are good, our daily work load resumes and very few relationships are maintained over time. I have learned from top level executives that building relationships are key to securing business transactions. Many times contracts are not awarded or even available right away, sponsorship budgets are not always a turnkey situation, and businesses are constantly accessing their initiatives, and the subsequent business opportunities that prevail go to those businesses who have found a way to evolve with the process. I have learned from my friend Denise Pines over the years. She is one of the most successful, congenial and humble people that I know, given the enormous success that she has had. Even when mounting star studded, media intensive events, sometimes it has taken a three to five-year process of building a relationship with a corporation before they released major dollars for the efforts that were in need of funding or a partnership.

What is your marketing & networking psyche? How do you perceive the process? I have developed a strategy called the 25/5 strategy. You go to that event and shine with all of your charisma. You may meet up to twenty-five networking contacts, but consider building a relationship with only five. I have traded the high volume for a more meaningful opportunity to cultivate awareness with a few. I have tried the other way and it hasn't worked. Another strategy to add to this is to ask the hard questions up front. Make sure that you are talking to the person who can help you or who can direct you to the person who can. How many of you have had the experience of vetting the wrong person in an organization and after several calls, meetings and proposals, you find out that they can't help you, all because it is out of their jurisdiction or realm of authority? So now you have invested time in a lead that has gone nowhere. You are out of the time and haven't made any money. Another question to consider has only occurred to me recently. Last year I attended an event with several major advertisers. Not only was I in the company of people who I would like to do business with, they were the heads of multi-cultural marketing divisions who could allocate budgets to a media outlet with whom I had an affiliation. I was over the moon with excitement. I met many great contacts, and traded information. A few months later after having been able to get only one of them on the phone I know that I should have asked another question. "After meeting today, how likely are you to return my call or respond to my correspondence or are you handing out business cards to be cordial?" Would I ask this? Yes, I would! Of course I would pepper this with charm, but as a business person I believe that there is great value in being able to communicate in an honest and direct manner. I also believe that like-minded business people can respect that. With the new attitude to boldly exist and with the new vision that you are the brand, you are encouraged to unapologetically and unequivocally get to the point when networking.

This advice is not designed to deplete the enjoyment of casual conversations and recreational events, but to challenge you to have a clear business purpose in mind when you are in the room with people who can potentially help you. I always recommend finesse and suggest an introduction like this:

"Hello, my name is _____ and I am excited about meeting or talking to the person in your company who reviews corporate proposals with a specific focus on _____ (then you name your focus). I have met a lot of people and I really want to make sure that I am presenting this to the right division so that I don't waste anyone's time. Are you that person at your company or can you direct me to the proper person?" And here's the addendum: "If you or someone in your company is not likely to respond for any reason, I won't be offended if you say so. I am excited to see if we can do business together but only if we can establish an open line of communication."

This approach sounds very direct. It is intended to be. It can be delivered with sincere warmth and a smile but get to the point. If this is not a potential business contact, make the decision to enjoy this person as a colleague or friend, but not to spend your valued business effort here. Since you are the brand that represents the brand, <u>you and your time</u> are just as valuable as the brand itself. Let this be a new idea about time management.

Step Four: Arrive more quickly at your decisions

This is for those of you who suffer from the paralysis of analysis. Nothing and no one in your organization can move until YOU do. In being the brand that stands beside the brand, there is both an inward and outward power shift. If you are in an organization with a multi-tiered power structure, then you may be bound by the chain of command. But what I'm referencing here is that area where you do have dominion. If you've been wanting to speak to your boss or your staff about a matter but have put it off, then do it now, or at the very least begin preparations for the most concise and respectful approach. If you have angst about the rate of pay that you are receiving from a paycheck or a client, make your counter offer now. Speak up! If you absolutely know that you have stayed in the same position for too long or tolerated an employee's shortcomings for too long, brace yourself to deal with it now. If you have a great staff that requires more training, then prepare to implement training now! Even if your decision is to set a timeline, then you have moved from contemplation into action. If your business requires a move but you are fearful of the cost factor, then start looking, if only for cost comparisons. I know of too many instances where desire was met with opportunity, and the business end worked itself out. This prompt to take action, is not designed to take the place of strategic planning, team building and good, plain common sense, but it is designed to invigorate those of you who languish (and you know who you are), and before you know it another year has gone by and you've been thinking and not doing. I have a saying: "Are you talking about what you're doing, or are you doing what you're talking about?" Now that global communications and business transactions occur at lightning speed and in real time, while you're making up your mind, someone else has closed a deal and moved on. You can no longer linger in the valley of indecision. What are you waiting for?

In re-adjusting your thinking, and now viewing yourself as a brand, ask yourself what must you do to reposition your brand? What new terminology must I add to my business vocabulary? Today words like search engine, social media, digital media, CPM, cost per click, mobile advertising, ads across all screens, Google analytics, QRS codes, and Google ad words are common place. Do you at lease have a cursory knowledge of what these words mean and how they affect the global economy? You don't have to become an expert but find out about the above mentioned and use it to grow your brand or understand more about how other brands use this information to grow their brands.

Step Five: Support outward decisions, with inward maintenance.

As you are making decisions about realigning your brand, make a commitment to cultivate, reinforce or secure your decisions by providing an atmosphere that supports your new mindset. In other words, it's time to nix the fear.

New thoughts, ideas or plans can easily be thrown off track when they have not taken root. Your new state of mind is like a seed that must be fertilized with quiet time, reading material and the support of like-minded people. Merely grasping a concept without further study will not optimize your experience or your outcome. You are encouraged to go for it! Really take the plunge to sharpen your tools.

Let's take branding for instance. Digital technology has changed the landscape in both the business and personal arena forever. There are few topics that cannot be further explored by simply clicking the mouse on your computer or the prompt on your digital devise. A few years ago when I had reached the apex of my existing resources, I decided to launch my own Research & Development department against all odds. The phone was simply not ringing anymore at Shall Be Productions aka SB Music, Media and Marketing. Every now and then I would get inquiries about marketing a small business or an independent book client. Even with them, I wanted to know how to better serve them. How could I make my service more cutting edge? I was also not getting as much response as I thought that I should from my job search. It was time for me to re-invest in my greatest asset, which was me! I searched for inexpensive or free webinars. I discovered a wealth of information that was available just by going to You Tube and entering the words "how to" followed by my desired subject matter. I also was made aware of KhanAcademy.com, Ask.com, AskJeeves.com and many more sites that opened a world of free information. Of course, each source and offering should be evaluated on its own merits, but there was a world of free information at my fingertips. Additionally, I found that I could search for bloggers on any topic, sign up for free newsletters or join networking groups on almost any subject matter. Next, I put reading back on the agenda. The local library became a destination once more. I was feeding off of more and more knowledge. It was like getting a mental tune up and it was empowering.

As a brand that stands beside the side, you are much more valuable when you have invested in yourself. In times of stiff competition to get a job, a client or a customer, you are a greater asset when you have expanded your pool of knowledge. Your outward decision is supported by constantly increasing your knowledge pool and it is maintained by centering yourself with a clear focus on your vision as a vital part of all that you do, and whatever entities that you are a part of.

Step Six: Devise a strategy

There is an African proverb that says: "Strategy is better than strength." To go the distance, you must have a strategy or a plan of action with systematic benchmarks.

First make a list of 5 goals for you or your business. When it comes to setting goals, sometimes it is intimidating because the idea of the goal is cluttered by thoughts of how you might achieve it, or how difficult or even impossible it is. Pace yourself, these are only thoughts and right now you are only committing these thoughts to a written goal. A famous singer once told me a word of wisdom from her grandmother. It simply said: "You eat a big elephant in chunks." I never forgot it and ask you to consider it now. Let's take the big elephant, and divide it into five sections or goals. We're not solving the entire problem or process, just committing to writing them down.

1. Collateralize it

Now that some goals are written down, let's take action steps. Collateralize it. In the marketing and promotions world artwork, posters, banners, bookmarks and other such items are referred to as collateral. What collateral can you create based on the goals that you want to achieve? If they are personal goals such as exercise or spend more time with family, or get to work earlier then even these goals can have some collateral associated with it. Make yourself a motivational poster and place it somewhere within constant eyesight where you can see if often. If the goals are business oriented, then create collateral for them as well. If the goal is to establish new sales leads, consider business cards with space to write in appointments on the back, or create new business cards that announce a talent or skill that you are not commonly known for. If you are introducing a new product or service, then consider making fliers that you pass out to friends, family or anyone else that you meet. You may also announce your new talent, skill or service electronically. Add the info to the signature of your personal or business email account. The point is people believe what they see. Make sample products or when possible, take pictures of past work that has not yet been documented in any formal manner.

You can also collateralize your goals by creating a logo, a brochure, a website or a placard with your new job title on it. I wouldn't suggest placing it on your desk just yet unless you are self-employed but you are creating energy around that which you hope to achieve. If you're an employee, you may or may not be able to automatically get a new title attached to your name but you can communicate to your boss whatever your enhanced skill set happens to be. You could say: Boss, for your information, I am also very skilled in social media, web design, conflict resolution, event planning, floral design, data recovery, etc. Whatever it is, you are calling attention to another level of your competency, which can only strengthen your brand. If you haven't yet figured a specific direction for your new concept of being the brand beside the brand, then at least print out a power statement on your computer and frame it or tape it on the wall! Every time you see it, it will inspire you and remind you that you not only see yourself differently, but you are requiring that the world do the same. There is a saying that goes: "Seeing is believing." Some goals or categories may have little evidence of what you have achieved. When that is the case, then your collateral can be a "To Do" list, an engraved piece of jewelry with your personal challenge inscribed on it or anything that can be printed, posted or created that will be a reminder and an inspiration of the action items associated with your goals.

2. Time it

How many times have you talked about doing something and then before you know it weeks, and even months have gone by? One of the actions that changed my life was when I not only gave myself deadlines, but when I treated my own deadlines the same way that I regarded others. I have a saying that simply says: "Face your own insanity." It's a humorous quip that challenges us to be realistic about both how brilliant and silly we can be at times. The minute our boss drops a deadline on us, then it's all hands on deck until it's achieved. What about if our loved ones have an emergency, we will drop everything to give them our full attention! It's a no-brainer. Well, set a time frame for talking to your boss, getting new business cards, coming up with a power statement, seeking new clients. Whatever it is, put a time frame on it. Don't be afraid that you won't make the mark. Goals un-set are goals un-met.

3. Press it

You have identified goals, you have collateral supporting those goals and a time frame for achieving them. Now let's take the written word a step further. Press it! Is there a story angle or anything newsworthy about who you are or what you have done or are striving to achieve? Can you create a weekly or monthly email with tips or updates? Can you or someone you know write a press release alerting the media about a goal or accomplishment? These days, digital media is dominant, but there are still hundreds of local newspapers in print that may be delighted to publish a story about you or something special that you bring to your business or corporation. We will expound on more ways to do this in the next section. You can also let your voice be heard by writing a letter to the editor. Blogging is another way to draft a consistent method around your desired goal and it can give you a brand name for being a connoisseur of your desired goal or topic. Being published provides another level of legitimacy. It may not guarantee your status as an expert on the subject by all who encounter you, but it will instill your committed voice to the topic. Should you amass a large and loyal following, then the numbers will lend themselves as a popular vote for who you are and what you have to say, and thereby solidify that you are an expert, at least to some. Either way, you are now out of your head, and on to the page (or blogosphere) with a portion of your goals, which is another giant step in being the brand beside the brand.

4. Pitch it

Once your brand is noted on paper, then pitch it. See if a local reporter wants to interview you about your cause or expertise. It's not a farfetched idea. Have you ever seen the nightly news and observed coverage of someone who has been a bird watcher for 50 years, or won a pie baking contest or someone who contacted the media to help them raise funds for a worthy cause? It could happen to you. Is your expertise tied into something that you can teach to others? For starters you can volunteer your services to senior citizens, community centers or youth groups. This will give you a chance to perfect your presentation. Then test it out as a workshop for pay. Can you offer your expertise as a consultant? The idea of pitching puts you in sales mode. For some this may be a very comfortable posture, but for others it may require some adjustments. Some may not be comfortable talking about themselves or what they can do. They might find it pretentious or boastful. For years I had an aversion to ever being referred to as a salesperson. I had an old picture in my head of the man who goes door-to-door, and when the proprietor opens the door he drops a wad of dirt on the rug, followed by a fast talking sales pitch for the latest vacuum cleaner. That picture lingers and so do the words that my aunt Mary used to say: "Beanie, you've got to toot your own horn." After many years, some successes and many failures, I finally understand what she means. Also after reading the works of many great men such as Napoleon Hill, Dennis Kimbro, Zig Ziglar, John H. Johnson, Reginald Lewis and Og Mandino (author of The Greatest Salesman In The World), I now acquiesce that life *always* hands us opportunities to present who you are and what you can do. It's up to us to polish our pitch and take the mystery out of it. Added to my most recent list of great business persons are Simon Sinek (author of Start With Why and Leaders Eat Last) and John C. Maxwell (author of Developing The Leader Within You, The Laws of Leadership and many more). By studying these and other great leaders you will gain tactics that are best suited to you. For now, it's okay that your pitch is not perfect, but practice it so that it flows like a deep desire to solve a problem, not sell a product, which thereby provides a great opportunity to create a pre-sold customer. This is another proven tactic of great business people. I'll also throw in a tip from my career as an actress. I can't tell you how exciting it was to prepare for television shows such as General Hospital, ER, Seinfeld and The Fresh Prince of Belair. One trick of the trade that was key for me was to remember that acting is not just rehearsing your lines so that you speak on cue, but acting is listening, yes actually listening to what the other person has to say. By hearing them you can respond sincerely with a solution to the need that they have expressed. The actor and the salesperson both have an audience that can either tune in or tune out depending on the presentation. When you have successfully tuned in to the person you are speaking to or pitching, then you have a better chance of drawing them in. Hard sells may lead to a quick close but do you want customers who are coerced or convinced? Adapt what works best for you in the long term, but sincerity never goes out of season.

5. Follow through with it

The best thing that you can do now that you are carving your own brand identity, is to stick with it and follow through with it. There is no going backward. Even if you make adjustments, you should see them as a course correction, and not an abandonment of the mission. You must adapt a mindset of completion. If you are fully launching a new business, then decide upon your levels of action. Also consider what is most feasible and place your larger goal into attainable segments. Is your first step to merely establish that you are seeking work, clients or recognition for a new skill set? Are you repositioning how you conduct business by performing an old skill set, one that people are familiar with but have not had to go through any particular or professional course of action? Are you the person who fixes everyone's computer as a favor but now you want to conduct it as a business? Are you the person who brings the best cakes and pies to family events, but now you are transitioning into professional baking services? I once worked for a company that had been newly acquired by a corporation. It was a neighborhood bake shop. The food was good, the service was satisfactory but the infrastructure was weak, with many vulnerable areas such as accounting, administration and overall operations. When the new corporate partners came in, half of the staff left. They feared change and the structure that the new owners brought to the table. The company made many changes internally, and worked hard to keep the quality of goods and integrity of the home baked menu that made the company so popular when it was run by a single person. However, the corporate infrastructure enabled the business to grow to a larger location, increase revenue and implement standards and best practices for their employees. Bottom line, there may be some knee jerk reactions along the way. Perhaps your new brand identity causes for a shift in the way that your present employer or colleagues view you. Relax and grow with the experience. Some level of discontent has inspired a curiosity about reaching the next level. With these steps and a commitment to press forth, you are changing the impression others have on you, by changing the impression you have of yourself. Keep at it until someone recognizes your value and agrees to promote, publicize or support your new found identity, purpose and product.

Let's also consider the financial aspect. With branding or re-branding yourself, there are undoubtedly a number of elements that require a financial investment and the option for short term or long term commitment. Whether it's as simple as ordering new business cards or brochures, building a website or paying for vending space at trade shows. There are costs. Are you considering leasing office space for a year, do you need a customized service vehicle or are you contemplating how to staff your new business? Either way, the costs can stack up and cause for a shocking profit/loss statement. The shock is good if you exceed expectations and the shock is bad if you invest more than you can afford to lose, and you do not recoup your investment when you expected. Everything can go down the drain pretty quickly. Here is where I advise you to separate the emotional connection to your dream, with the hard, cold and fast rules of business. Devise a time line and stick to it. If you have not hit your financial benchmark by a certain time, plan for an exit strategy. This does not mean failure! This means that you exit from that exact method of execution of your goal or business, then re-structure how you can continue under more cost efficient measures. If you leased an office in a high rise building in the middle of the corporate pulse of town, then have a downsizing approach already planned as part of your exit strategy. Can you operate the same business a few blocks away for less? How about doing business online or by appointment only? My point is that an exit strategy is a key factor for success because it calls for full scale business planning out the gate.

Should you acquire investors, they will be concerned about your ability to make money, achieve a return on their investment and not lose their money in the end. Dreams can be nourished forever, but business and financial goals are time-sensitive.

If you are able to identify when you need to shift your approach, then this is indeed a quality that will ensure your ability to follow through to achieve success. In the aviation world, it is quite common to hear pilots say that they adjust their altitude to avoid turbulence. We also hear the dreadful term, crash and burn. Dreams, goals and business plans can crash and burn when there is no foresight for how the market might shift and no contingency plan that can provide an alternate way to do business or approach your goal, while maintaining your financial footing in the interim. Though you may have faith in your abilities and potential for success, it is important to assess your belief system versus the realities of your day-to-day business. Pay attention to the marketplace, do not further jeopardize your financial situation because you have held on to one manner of doing business for too long. Follow through, but follow through with as much information and strategy that is available to you.

Step Seven: Insist on name brand identity

Humility is an admirable quality for it is the antithesis of egocentrism. In the past, it has not been looked upon favorably if an employee's own esteem seems to parallel or replace the initiatives of the company. The ubiquitous team spirit was the preeminent effort to attain. It became the all-encompassing theme for getting the job done, and in the end "the company" gets the credit, except for some occasions where a few people are singled out for their efforts. I say to you that if you are in a company or running a business that has guaranteed job security for at least twenty years and a benefit package that can sustain you well into retirement, then skip to the end of this book. Congratulations: "You Won!" However, if you are like most people in the workforce, the security that we used to experience from employment or awarded contracts is not and will never be the same. Therefore, the mindset of the all-encompassing "team" must also never be the same. Incorporate the same vigor that it takes to be a great team player into your re-adjusted approach to branding yourself and your talents.

Maintain a high regard for company policies, embrace every opportunity to affirm who you are and what you bring to the table. Get your credit whenever and wherever you can. If there is a company newsletter, offer to write about what it is that you discovered, how you implemented a strategy, led a taskforce, hosted an intervention, bridged a gap, avoided a crisis or any number of ways that you specifically led a change effort in the organization. Of course give credit to your team, your supervisor, your Vice President, whomever should share the accolades for whatever the accomplishment was. If there is a public relations or media department in your organization, offer to get this information to them or ask to be interviewed. Yes, I said ASK to be interviewed. I realize that these tendencies are not the norm but the days of sitting back and hoping to be noticed, rewarded or promoted for exemplary work are long gone. This is not about being self-centered but self-actualized or activated. I offer this as a strategy for success and not something that is merely motivated by ego or the need for fame. There is a difference. As a business person you will be granted work opportunities from two circumstances only. Either people know you or the brand that you represent, or they decide to give you a try. In either case, the more evidence that you can produce to substantiate your claims of excellent products or services, the better your chances for acquiring the work, contract or customers that you seek. The very foundation of this advice is to shift the paradigm where you are not looking for the "work," but rather the "work" is looking for you because you have aligned yourself (or re-aligned yourself) so that your reputation precedes you. With that, I reinforce that you insist on name brand identity, meaning *your name*, alongside the brand, every time you represent the brand itself.

I'll give you an example of a business associate who bought advertising from a local radio station. Each year he had a client who purchased about $150,000 of commercial activity during tax season. My friend's client had brought some new associates on board, who did not know the protocol of sales and advertising as it related to sales commission. The newbies contacted the radio station and purchased $30,000 worth of radio commercials with a new salesman at the radio station. My friend had not made it clear to the client that all ad sales should be handled by him. So because the client's new associates made a direct buy from the radio station, they did not get the best rate, my friend lost the benefit of his agency commission and the sales rep who usually handled that particular tax account was also left out of any due commission.

Was this with ill intentions? Probably not, but a clear case where a lack of communication and flat out insistence on brand name identity proved to be costly. Many times we lose out because we assume that people will automatically know to give us credit, or know that we represent a particular account or that we initiated a dialogue that ended up with someone else closing the deal.

Here's another example of what can happen when you fail to insist on brand name identity. In 1994 I had the great fortune of starring in a short film directed by Kim Fields, the adorable Tootie from the NBC sitcom The Facts of Life, and it ran from 1978 to 1988 for those of you who are old enough to remember. Kim was an accomplished actress who began as a child star and later became a regular fixture on TV and film. She went on to direct over 70 episodes on network television including Fox's Living Single and Nickelodeon's Keenan and Kel. This is how we met. Kim spotted me in a stellar moment when I appeared in a stage production of For Colored Girls by Ntozake Shange. I would NEVER admit to such back in the 1990's but it's a new day yes, I can truly say that I was in the zone as I portrayed the Lady In Red. That performance at the Estelle Harmon Theater in Hollywood led to another tremendous blessing. Miss Fields was about to produce her directorial debut, a short film titled "Silent Bomb." She saw me in the play and was so impressed that she waited to meet me one night after the show. She said that she had a special role in mind for me. I auditioned and won the lead role of a police officer who contracted HIV from a blood transfusion. Due to Kim's brilliant directing and her excellent production team, we pulled off a quality piece of work. A few months later the film was nominated for an award at the late Mayme Clayton's BACS awards (produced by The Black American Cinema Society). The awards ceremony drew an A-list of Hollywood elite, including directors, producers, casting directors, you name it. On the big night at the Directors Guild in Hollywood, the theater was packed. On my row was the legendary actress Pam Grier and the famous directors The Hudlin Brothers; one of which later directed The Academy Awards.

On the night in question, it was time for the Best Director Award. They showed the clip of our film, which featured a scene by me, the leading lady. The film won. Kim thanked her Director of Photography by name, a few others by name and the rest of the accolades went to her "cast and crew." That's it. That's all. My heart sunk. To have my name mentioned among such powerhouses would have been invaluable. Kim is a nice and congenial person, who probably gave no thought to it. At the time I was not of the mindset that I must insist on name brand identity. I left it to chance. Showbiz agents fight for credits for their clients. There is great jockeying for where an actor's name will be placed on the screen and on other promotional matter relative to a film production, playbill or television show. A bit wise too late, I now understand the politics of the industry. My story ends with a Hollywood twist sprinkled by two superstars at the time. The night of the award show I felt crocodile tears about to press through, so I had to quickly get out of there before the after party began. As I waited for my car in the valet area, a well-known actor approached me in his typical Hollywood cool demeanor. He puffed a few times from his cigarette, blew off the smoke and said in his deep and raspy voice: "I like your work." Surprised, I asked him: 'You know my work?' He replied: "I saw your work, on the screen tonight." He puffed again and asked: "What's your name?" Relieved and validated, I nobly said: 'My name is LaRita Shelby.' Thankfully my car had arrived because the tears were about to fall. As I left the heart of Hollywood headed through the curves of the famous Laurel Canyon Boulevard, it occurred to me that I had just had a conversation with Laurence Fishburne. At least "he" knew my name. Next was a trip to my good friend Blair Underwood's house, who recalled a similar story early in his career. With brotherly advice, he assured me that I was not alone in this, and that going forth I would have to insist that my name not fall through the cracks. Now, I am challenging you to do the same.

Think of your favorite sports team. Borrow from some of the bravado. Lean towards confidence versus arrogance and become your own brand ambassador and MVP (most valuable player). When you think of the Los Angeles Lakers who comes to mind? What about the Dallas Cowboys? If you had to hire an athlete who would you hire? The same holds true for any profession. If you had to hire someone, would you prefer someone who you have heard of and has already built a reputation that you trust?

This strategy is designed to help you build a presold customer and the benefactor is you. Have you ever gotten an oil change for your automobile, and then have a sticker placed on your vehicle with the company logo on it, as well as your oil change info? Why didn't they leave out the logo and just put the date of the oil change? Because they wanted you to remember from whom you got the service, so that when it's time to return they can ensure that you are a repeat customer.

I know that in every work scenario it is not possible to single out your contributions to the overall team effort. Persons with contract positions with Hallmark, Disney, other defense, I.T. and design companies may have strict nondisclosure codes and policies which restrict ownership or disclosure of what individual work is done in conjunction with them. This book recommends absolute compliance where these practices are enforced. However, pursue whatever is in the realm of possibilities where you can make sure that you are properly credited for the work that you do. In some cases, you can verbalize or put in writing exactly how you would like your work to be credited.

For example, I have another associate who had helped to promote a major event that attracted thousands of attendees. He had negotiated only a modest compensation and he derived much enjoyment from the work that he did for the organization, still each year he was desirous of attracting new business. After sharing with him my brand beside the brand strategy, he has now negotiated to have a full page ad in the program book that goes to the ten thousand plus attendees. The ad consists of info about his company and the array of services that he provides. Again, I stress that the intent is not to take away from the brand, but to position yourself beside the businesses, events, products and services that have benefitted from your great work.

Another example of how we see this daily, is when uniformed workers wear a name plate right on their uniform. It is usually beside or beneath the brand name. This kind of identity personalizes the service of the employee who proudly stands beside the brand.

The point is that you are just as important as what you do for the company. Own it, remember it, insist on it and use it as a tool that will create a good reputation for yourself as well as the company that you represent. How can a potential customer call upon you if they don't know your name? You simply cannot wait for customers to find you anymore. You must insist on brand name identity to be the brand that stands beside the brand.

Other ways of being the brand beside the brand and insisting on brand name identity is to place yourself at events where your product or service is sold or exposed.

Instead of just delivering products to an event, seize opportunities to meet and greet those who will benefit from your product. Again, when and where possible and where protocol allows. Do you have a product that can be identified by stickers on the product, printed ribbons or packaging letting customers know that you designed the promotional items or can you place a name plate in front of your famous ice carving at the wedding reception? Can you negotiate to carve off a few dollars from the bill if your business cards can be prominently placed near your items at private or corporate events?

Can you accompany your company at events where TV, radio and social media coverage are provided? Can you offer to be the company spokesperson? Can you volunteer to write an article or blog on the company website or for a non-profit organization whose audience may need your information? How can you make effective use of the media and position yourself as the brand beside the brand? As a media and marketing professional, I have personally been involved with designing media campaigns for major brands who wanted to highlight some facet of their company's community outreach, diversity or global citizenship. To do this best would include a tactic that humanized the company, or gave it a personal appeal instead of just a corporate entity that provided a product or a service. The information imparted can endear their consumer base, because they can now see a company that cares about them and not just about the money that they spend with them. We did this for several campaigns on EURweb.com, home of the Electronic Urban Report. We ran a sponsored content campaign for Verizon Wireless in order to raise awareness for their Hope Line program, whereby they collect old cell phones to donate to victims of domestic violence. We interviewed and featured Verizon's Manager of Multicultural Communications and Community Relations. In doing so we accomplished three things. We put Verizon in our headline news, we raised brand awareness of how they support the community AND we presented the manager as a valuable member of the Verizon team. She became the brand beside the brand. Verizon serves 94 million customers but whenever I think of Verizon, I think of this person in particular. If I see her outside of context of Verizon, I still think of her as someone who is an expert in Multi-Cultural Communications and Community Relations. With her having her own brand name identity, it does not take away from the fact that she is (or was at the time of publication) a part of the Verizon team. For me, it ADDS to the fact that she is a part of that team, because I feel connected to real people who are capable of providing a service, and also care about me and the things that I care about. We have also done this with other brands such as McDonalds, Northrop Grumman and more.

You should also seek opportunities to speak and sell. Your brand name identity is in the presentation that you deliver, and you should have ample products at the back table near the door.

It is a competitive world out there whether you've developed the latest tech app or if you bake cookies, competition is everywhere. It is in your best interest to seek to generate twice the exposure than you would have in recent years.

Step Eight: Insist on your value.

"Is someone making withdrawals from your intellectual capitol?"

A companion strategy to name brand identity is the insistence on your value. This holds true especially for small businesses and entrepreneurs who set their own costs for goods and services. Because of the size of your business, you are much closer to the bottom line cost or profit/loss analysis. You have more leverage in adjusting your profit margins to remain competitive and to acquire new business. This is a benefit. However, the drawback is that many times in the end you make concessions just to get the business, or assist the customer who has inadequate finances. This can be great for building brand awareness, but it can have you deadlocked for gaining the type of accounts and profits that will help your business to grow exponentially.

When you're just starting out in business most of your customers will be people that you know and they know that you have a personal interest in their success. I entered the business world as an entertainer who had a background in broadcast media. Because of my expertise there, one by one I was solicited to assist with the promotions and marketing of community organizations, followed by friends who were branching out in the small business arena. My first projects were labors of love, which became more and more time consuming. I admit it was exciting to see events that I had packaged and pitched to the media result in being covered by the press or to see large dollars come in from corporations for non-profit organizations for whom I had written proposals and solicited funds. It was not fun however when I hosted my own events and was in dire need of in-kind support, only to witness that my events were poorly attended and underfunded. It was a sad and shocking reality. I had gone the distance for others, but sold myself short, assuming that mutual reciprocity would prevail.

Then there was also the fact that I was tracking countless hours away from my own pursuits to assist in the dreams or goals of others. Don't get me wrong, charity has its place and its rewards, but I was not in the business of charity. A portion of my time and life will always be dedicated to giving back, but time and time again my expertise was called upon in order to contribute to someone else's success. This was expertise that had taken me years to develop. I invested time in trial and training to navigate marketing, media, and PR initiatives. I was also calling upon relationships in the business and civic arena that had also taken me years to build and I was giving all of this away for free. If I did receive a stipend, by the time I divided how much time I was putting into the project, the pay would have amounted to $7 or $8 an hour, or less!

This was not a matter of my heart's intentions, but where my good business sense was taking me. With the shift in the economy I was not pulling down huge dollars from major contractors. My television and film work had nearly dried up and I had no major radio contracts, but more and more I was called upon in the marketing and media arena. It was a clear case of one door closing and another one opening wide before me. Though I did not have fortune 500 marketing experience yet, what I had was just what new business owners needed. They did not have fortune 500 budgets and did not need a fortune 500 marketing plan, they needed someone that they trusted to help them get started. Here is where my broadcast media experience came in. I could speak the language of media sales, however think like a consumer and approach campaigns as a business owner. As an actress who worked on major ad campaigns for McDonalds, ReMax Realtors and other brands, I witnessed the discussions of the creative team, the producers, the directors and the clients, as they hashed over every detail of how a product would be presented and how every word should be shaped regarding the product image or the company message. I was familiar with writing and producing radio commercials, as well as short and long form programming. As a former Public Service Director at a Los Angeles radio station, I had seen numerous public service campaigns submitted to the station. When I transitioned from being an announcer to the Chief Journalist of Lee Bailey's Radioscope (an hour long syndicated news program) suddenly I had an even broader insight into how companies pitch their projects to the media. I was on the receiving end of news releases from The White House, major television and movie studios, publishing houses, and every sort of pitch seeking coverage from the press. While at first I lamented having to hash through so much information to select the ten interviewees that we featured each week, in the long run, it was educational for me. I had first hand comparative analysis that would be valuable to my future clients.

Additionally, I had a thirst for knowledge. I was accepting that the old business models were dying out. Many qualified people that I knew had fallen outside of the talent pool; their skill sets were not as much in demand. I personally knew the horror of hunting for work, sifting through endless online applications, thumbing through stacks of business cards (yes, business cards) only to find out that the people who were once in influential positions could no longer help me because they were either unemployed themselves or were biting their nails in fear that they could be laid off at any time.

Still I was blessed to have continuous calls from people who sought some facet of what I could deliver as a marketing, branding and media professional. The ball was in my court to assign a value to it.

The first phase of insisting on your value involves you verbalizing what you do, then itemizing it preferably in print on a contract, brochure or memo. Next decide upon a price for a package deal or itemize which services are available and at what price point. Of course if you're starting out you may discount some price items because you are still exploring and balancing out what services require a certain amount of time. Yes, there will be unforeseen circumstances that require additional time or services to get the job done. All of this is par for the course. However, start with something that assigns a value for the time and talent that you are providing to your customer. Many times it requires some adjustments as you educate (or re-educate) people on your value, especially if you're now asking people to consider paying for services that they may have gotten from you or someone else for free.

I have a simple phrase for you to remember and tell your reluctant friends, family and customers. "Treat me like the chicken!"

Now what could this possibly mean in a serious business book about branding? It's all in reassessing your personal value and communicating it to others. I came up with this humorous saying after many years of working as an entertainer. Time and time again I was approached by well-meaning event planners and independent producers. They wanted the actors or entertainers to show up and perform for free or for little or nothing. Most of the time a performer is purely driven by passion and will accept the offer to share their gift or to gain exposure. But with maturity comes a certain level of expertise, and there is a value added to that. I started to think. Hmmm, at all of these events the planners meet with the hotel to reserve the room. Then they strike up a contract with the banquet department and agree upon the fees to be paid in advance for the dinner (and it's usually a chicken dinner). If they sell tickets, they build their profit into the price of the tickets but one thing is for certain, the chicken gets paid for off the top! No matter how worthy the cause or the size of the benefit concert, the CHICKEN gets figured into the budget FROM THE START! So I came up with this message to all of my future clients and bookers, "TREAT ME LIKE THE CHICKEN." The chicken is not bought on a contingency, whether it is baked, fried, roasted, stuffed, sauced, skewered or bar-b-que, the chicken makes it into the budget. So from hence forth, as a business professional, I want you to say unashamed and with boldness: "Treat me like the chicken!"

All humor aside, I believe that it is important to teach people how it is that you want to be treated or valued. For many of us, it requires re-educating our client base as to where we are now, or where we wish to go. Okay, let's be totally honest here. No matter what your business is, if it's tax preparation, home improvement, real estate appraisal, legal services you name it, you have quite possibly gotten a call when your expertise was needed but because you were a friend or a relative the caller wasn't expecting to pay you anything at all for your services.

In my most familiar circles I refer to this as the 'help me out, do me a favor, cut me some slack' scenario. The first couple of times it happens, most of us are obliged to do a favor. It's great to do good deeds, but repeated calls in this manner sends the wrong signal, especially if your area of expertise is your business or livelihood and you are reliant upon your skills as a revenue stream. Again, this is not referring to what you have designated to do as part of your volunteer work or community service. I'll use myself as an example here. For as much as I had gained a wellspring of entertainment industry knowledge before producing my first project, I was clueless as to how much I really should have had as far as a marketing budget was concerned. When I called upon the industry elite for favors, I was quickly made aware that their services were indeed available but at a price! I was calling upon people who had invested years at numerous record labels and they had built invaluable relationships at radio and even retail outlets. I had to learn that in business, most of the time you have to pay to play. The onus of building my dream was not on them. It was up to me to earn, raise or borrow the necessary capital to properly pursue my dream as a business. That alone helped motivate me to quickly assign a higher value to my time and talent, and insist on it.

Remember I am writing this book on the heels of successes and failures, and I am willing to be transparent. After failing to turn a profit on my investments, I was even more hungry to find out how to win, how to get better at what I do and to come face to face with all that I know and all that I did not know. I digested as many seminars and webinars that I could afford. As the great motivational speaker Les Brown says "Whatever you're seeking, is seeking you." Putting in more and more time to learn from my own mistakes and sharpen my intellectual tools gave me the confidence to make the next bold statement: "I inspire for free, I inform for a fee."

Say it with me, "I inspire for free, I inform for a fee."

You must educate your customer or audience on the value of both. Inspiration comes from deep within. It's the power to stimulate the heart and soul and incite confidence and action in those that you inspire. It is an honor and it is even humbling to have this effect on someone. I give it generously because it has generously been given to me. Information on the other hand has been quite costly to acquire, either it came from the school of hard knocks or from investing countless hours of studying and seeking knowledge, it was not given to me for free and now as a business person with a renewed consciousness about my value, my information is no longer free. I can tell you that *"you can do it"* for no cost at all! If you ask me to show you *"how"* then I must tap into my intellectual capital for that, and you can't pay off school loans or build a start-up business on motivation and appreciation alone, it takes money. We now live in the information age. Everything hinges upon how fast information moves. Knowledge is power, learning power is earning power, therefore once more I say; *"I inspire for free and I inform for a fee."*

Just try it, or at the very least cordon off those customers (or friends) who will continue to receive the friends and family rate. Then plan to vigorously go after additional clients at a new price point; one that is in sync with your new assessment of your values, your goals and your worth. I encourage anyone who struggles in this area to take a look at your finances, your resources and your profit/loss statement. Your time counts as a resource. If you're losing time, you're losing money. Speak up, communicate to your friends, family and clientele that you have realigned your product and service offerings and you will now be available at a certain time frame for a certain fee. I must caution you that it may take some adjustments because now here you are insisting on your value, when your friends, family and some of your customers have been used to getting you for free, or for a discount. Well, give yourself a raise and take yourself off of the sales rack! The deeply discounted you is discontinued. You are no longer stacked on the shelf with items that have no price tag. Draw the line and insist on your value from now on.

Step Nine: Commit to expanding your turf

How often do you mingle in the same circles? Does your business networking cycle consist of the same people at the same venues, and have you engaged in these same circles for years and years, with the exception of an occasional convention or two?

My first job out of college was at a local radio station that played R&B music. Because of the format at that time in history it was referred to as black radio. My first convention was The BRE, the Black Radio Exclusive. I connected with other professionals who worked in black radio across the country. We also interfaced with executives who worked in black music divisions at major record labels. From there as I started to work in TV and film, most of the time I got cast to work on black shows, meaning shows that were predominately populated by African American cast members and story lines, although there were some exceptions. My networking pool consisted of people of various ethnicities, but they specialized in products aimed at a certain audience. The upside of this was what later became industry driven initiatives for diversity and inclusion. The term urban was forthcoming in the 1990's. This term encompassed a majority African American audience and could include Latinos, and in some cases inner city Asians. However, in my world, it mostly referred to young, hip African American culture. It encompassed a confluence of ideas and strategies to reach a particular audience, which was anything other than the "majority" or general market.

Over time, I became a specialist in urban media. I am proud of the expertise that I amassed because it is of great value to understand the delicacies in marketing a message, product or service that is culturally specific. One false move can backfire, though it may be well intentioned. Cultural identity is important and so are businesses who focus their products are services within this arena. But remaining in a cultural niche can be stifling especially if your businesses has ceased to grow. Let's face it, businesses exist to make money and money crosses cultural lines. If you are a business owner or individual who works in a certain industry that caters to all types of people (also referred to as the general market) and you only network with one particular group of professionals or one ethnic group, then you are shut off from a wealth of knowledge and an area of potential growth in your consumer base. The challenge here is for you to expand the market for your business and industry in order to gain a wider range of opportunities. You may question what it is that you have to offer but consider this, businesses work in tandem with other businesses. For example, if your business is bookkeeping and accounting, you may only see a need to network with other accountants, but people who run machine and tool companies need good bookkeeping and accounting. If you're the only accountant at a machinist convention, you have leveraged an opportunity. Often times people don't know that it's you that they need until they are face-to-face with you and realize that you are exactly that they have been looking for.

This happens quite frequently when you break away from the norm and go where others are afraid to go. It's like traveling The Way Of The Road Less Travelled (Peck, 1978). If you only hang with people who look like you, act like you and work like you, your circle is closed. If this circle produces all that you want and need, then fine I dare not argue with that. If you desire to grow, then you are missing an enormous potential for growth and expansion by sticking to your closed circle.

I remember when a good friend of mine had a new relationship with Microsoft. As a result, I was invited to many free workshops on Power Point, Excel, Quick Books and any number of new applications in Microsoft Office. This was back in the early 2000's and I was working mostly as a journalist and radio announcer at the time so I did not think that these things applied to me. I didn't feel the need to corroborate with the tech types or office types. Fast forward fifteen years later and I regret not stepping out of my comfort zone and acquiring the knowledge and the networking pool that had expertise in these areas when it was offered for FREE. Now I am engaged in 100% more desk top publishing, new business development and proposal writing than I was back then. I have had to complete RFP's (Requests for Proposals) with detailed spreadsheets and present power points. For sure I am functional on computers today, but I regret my missed opportunity. Many times other cultures (whether ethnic or occupational) will welcome you and seek to find out where there is a mutual benefit, especially if they are in business to make money, and trust me, they are in business to make money!

With the expansion of your turf also comes the opportunity to gather information and study markets. What trends are showing an economic impact? What products are on the rise? What products or services will be phased out in coming years based on market analysis? I say this because this is not something that I have always known to do myself.

I was immersed in people who were merely led by their passion, which is a good starting point but does it give you enough information to go the long run? I have another saying, a Jazzy Rita-ism and it goes like this: "Inspiration gets you going. Information keeps you going!" How often have you seen a business start with huge dollars spent on construction and design, and then see the same business vacate in a year or two? Perhaps the products and services were excellent, but what did the business owner know about the marketplace? What was the per capita income of the neighborhood? What was the foreclosure rate? Were jobs coming in or going out of the immediate area? What similar businesses came into the neighborhood and survived? What did they do to survive? How long were they in business? What relationships did they have in the community? How much did they spend on advertising? Did they even advertise? I know that not everyone who has survived entrepreneurship has asked these questions beforehand, but I submit to you that the climate of business in America and elsewhere else has changed forever! A hamburger stand or fancy coffee shop idea will never be new again. McDonalds and Starbucks are here to stay! Social media and online shopping are here to stay! The fact that the average consumer has multiple options to spend their disposable income is a never changing, ever growing reality. Even businesses in remote areas must (or at least should) study the cultural and consumer behavior of the environment before setting up shop, unless they are starting one of the mega-store franchises.

A few places where you can gather market data are: Marketsearch.com, ThinkwithGoogle.com, Forbes.com, MarketsandMarkets.com, BusinessNewsDaily.com, Curbed.com (for emerging trends in real estate), and a number of others. Confirmit.com offers a fact sheet for download free.

Cross check and get your own referrals before spending any money with any of these and by all means read the fine print. You should fully understand the exit clause on any subscription based services or services offered for hire. There is an upside and a downside to online companies. The downside is that anyone can have a spectacular website and make any number of promises. The upside is that their track record is also easy to research. If they have been credible or not, then their record or service can be tracked by a Google search of their name. While it is common for a few disgruntled customers to have a report somewhere, a trend of unsatisfactory service should be regarded. Places like ConsumerReports.org, Yelp.com and the Better Business Bureau are also excellent for tracking customer feedback. Keep this in mind when launching and maintaining your own business. Your customer or client's opinion about you is one key stroke away.

Expanding your turf also includes team building. The wider your network, the broader your reach and the more thorough your resources are, the greater your chances of survival. Starting now, expand your turf. You may do it in the terrestrial world by networking in different circles. You may begin immediately online by researching and connecting with professionals or potential alliances via social media. The great benefit of digital media and the internet is that now you can gain instant access with just one click of the mouse, the hardest part is expanding your mind. With that, let's assume that your mind is made up to venture into new territories, so get busy expanding your turf.

Step Ten: Reflect, Inspect and Project

Initiating any organizational change requires an assessment of how a company or entity came to be. It's kind of like a doctor acquiring a medical history even before an examination, despite the dull or gory symptoms. My approach is comprised of a three tier method where one must reflect, inspect and project. The process may evolve into several subdivisions.

The reflection stage is a healthy review of systems, processes, management styles, finances and human resources. Studying the history of you or your organization is important because it gives clues as to how change has occurred in the past. This information exposes strengths and weaknesses. An astute analysis can reveal vulnerabilities where no support system or exit strategy was in place. The reflection stage should also include a survey of marketplace activity that has both positively and negatively impacted you or your company's current position. All of this points to where changes should be made to re-boot, to maintain or to continue to grow.

By investing the time for a thorough analysis, the reflection stage should build a stronger foundation of confidence in yourself and hopefully a bond of confidence between you and the people who will be most impacted by the change. The reflection stage is likened to what Michael Tushman and Charles A. O'Reilly III call structural and cultural inertia (1996). Michael Tushman is a Professor of Business

Administration at Harvard Business School and Charles A. O'Reilly is a Professor of Human Resource Management and Organizational Behavior at the Graduate School of Business at Stanford University in California. Tushman and O'Reilly discuss their observations of Ambidextrous Organizations in an article in the Harvard Business Review (April 2004). They state that structural inertia causes organizations to be resistant to change because of the size, structure or complexity of the company. Meanwhile cultural inertia is stifling to a company's growth because the company is complacent due to past successes. Tushman and O'Reilly III also co-authored the book "Lead and Disrupt" (Stanford University Press 2016).

The reflection strategies were used when I landed a contract with 1 Plus One Management Inc., a boutique sized consulting, marketing and advertising firm based in Los Angeles. The owner has 30 years of corporate sales experience. He formed his own firm ten years ago. Since then he has had ongoing contracts from three clients who pay retainer fees and allocate a hefty advertising budget, from which the agency receives a percentage of the ad buys as commission. The company generates another 20% of its revenue from other clients and project based assignments. To date 1 Plus One has acquired business by referral only. The reflection stage allowed me to assess the strengths, vulnerabilities and opportunities within the organization. The strength of the company rested upon the fact that the company had consistently delivered a quality product and it had adhered to cultural sensitivities for clients who conducted business with the urban community, thereby building long lasting client relationships. To reflect on the job market and the global economy, I looked at the unemployment rate from the previous year. In the summer it was 8.20% and by December it had fallen to 7.80%. By March of the following year, the unemployment rate was at 7.60% with the estimated number of unemployed persons in the U. S. at about 11.7 million. This was reported by the Bureau of Labor Statistics at the time. A reflection of and understanding of the shifts in the economy helped the company to depersonalize its losses and recognize that when fewer people are working, there is less disposable income for all potential consumers. Reflecting on this information also helped us understand the driving force for companies to be more competitive in nature and superior in terms of their product and service offerings. With 1 Plus One, we simply could not expect that customers would come to us with hefty budgets in hand, or the same sized budgets as they did before the shift in the economy. Reflecting called for a refocus of how we would attract more clients and customers. The reflection stage is approached as something healthy, positive, empowering, and a necessary link to the next step.

Inspection can actually be interchanged with introspection here because we're dealing with a theme that causes a look inward to search the mechanics of a company, product or service. This is an internal look at yourself, your product or service and the people that you rely upon to drive your mission forward. This is where honesty and objectivity can also be a tool of empowerment. Now that we have reflected on what has gone on in the company and in the marketplace, this is where we also look within. As a person or as a staff of people, what is working well for you and what is repeatedly re-implemented though it fails to produce the desired results?

Many people and companies are accustomed to outside inspectors or licensing agents examining a business to see if they are up to a certain code or standard, but many businesses also fail to develop the same strategies in house. Oftentimes, it is not for a lack of desired excellence, it is because the pulse of the workflow churns at a status quo and so do the profits, until something implodes.

While inspecting internal practices, ask yourself how long does it take to get to the people or the information that you need? It may be time to ask the hard questions first. I have personally witnessed many "yes" men and women at organizations who are afraid to challenge or disagree with the senior authority, or they only do so to a point. Usually hard questions only offend those who are not forthcoming with credible information. Another strategy for strengthening and re-positioning your brand is to change how negative information is viewed. If the information can be discovered and corrected in house, then you have scored a team win which helps to maintain total quality management (TQM) and a competitive edge. Author and Neuro-Linguistic Practitioner Nicholas Boothman (2010) says: "The only time you can fail at something is when you stop processing feedback." (p. 269)

As a consultant and independent contractor, I have the great benefit of having worked on various sides of the industry. It strengthens my value because I bring clients a wholesome view of the product representative, the production department and the consumer. I encourage stakeholders to shift their view and consider all variables when planning for change, despite the reasons that prompted the change. "A regulatory, economic, competitive and or technical shift with the same organizational systems and processes do not work." (Nadler & Tushman, 1989, p.77)

The call for inspection is a collection of data that is consistent with V. G. Kondalkar's (Kondalkar, 2009, p.26) steps for organization development, which lists a diagnosis and fact finding stage, a system of identifying and correcting problems, and interventions.

Closer inspection of 1 Plus One Management revealed that we only offered on demand marketing, media placement and consulting services. By creating new divisions such as seasonal media, corporate training and speaker divisions, we could now solicit additional opportunities from new and existing clients. My inspection also found that we fully promoted the products of our clients, but there was no consistent promotional effort for our company. I implemented an immediate public relations component whereby we would treat company news with the same urgency as news from our paid clients. The result has brought coverage in two local newspapers that reported on the launch of our speaker's series and a profile of the company owner's thirty-year career. The goal is not mere self-promotion, but to cross promote our capabilities to attract new business. We have gained new customer interests, and we now have an affiliation with a major university that wants to funnel interns through our company. So, the more detailed the inspection, the more efficient the plans will be for all projections. Inspection is taking a look at what is, which takes us to the next step in making the case for change and for renewed branding.

Taking the leap forward requires a vision and a plan for it. This is where we project from where the previous steps have laid the foundation. Now that we know what was, we understand what is, we now have a vision for what must be. This is the launching pad for positive and profitable change. Projections must deploy urgency, clear instructions, proper training as well as realistic expectations for growth potential. Projection requires instrumental leadership as described by Nadler and Tushman in Beyond The Charismatic Leader (p. 84). The instrumental leader "focuses on the management of teams, structures and individual processes to create individual instrumentalities. It involves managing environments to create conditions that motivate the desired behavior. Anticipatory thinking is also referenced as a prerequisite for leadership development, as is defining managerial competence."

Michael Tushman & Charles A. O'Reilly III (1996) state that: "All relatively wealthy businesses can afford to explore new technologies" (p. 10). This quote appears in the California Management Review article "Ambidextrous Organizations: Managing Evolutionary and Revolutionary Change." The projection stage for 1 Plus One involved setting quarterly targets for new business and re-branding the company itself as a newsworthy entity that markets community based and national campaigns. I also encouraged the owner to strengthen the infrastructure by adding new technologies or applications. Currently we have increased our ability to mount digital media campaigns for our clients. By shifting our mindset, and working with experts like Google, we are now placing media for a budget that would have otherwise been allocated elsewhere. There are other technical shifts in the making.

Reflection can arm a client or company with information that endears them to the process of making changes because together we carefully assess the trials and triumphs that have brought them this far. Then we take a sincere look at all that is going on within the company from the products, processes and people who are involved. This inspection sets forth a schematic that points to where a company needs to go in order to maintain and grow. The projection is the exciting unveiling of either a well-planned vision or a focused restructuring that has been motivated by whatever forces that made the necessary case for an organizational change and creating a re-invigorated brand.

By identifying with a brand, you are humanizing the experience that you have with that brand. You can then add that experience as a form of credibility between you, the brand (whatever the product or service is) and the potential customer or client. You become the brand's voice of authority, pointing the consumer to something or someone that can solve a problem. You have seen this in action probably without ever even taking note of it. Have you ever gone to a restaurant, perused the menu, and then looked up still undecided and asked the waiter: "What do you suggest or which do you think is better?" At that moment that waiter is the brand beside the brand. Think about it. Part of who you are is in what you have designed, or in what you have experienced. Part of who you are is in what you are proposing, or what need you are seeking to fill. Whether you've already led teams in a corporation, worked at a local diner, or started a business, speak up with the confidence that you are the brand beside the brand.

Bonus: Dealing with difficult people

Every victory is not called right away. For the rest of your life you will have to deal with Kill joys, dream stealers, peace robbers, you name it. We might also call them jerks, jug heads, jilted and jaded. No matter what you do, they are going to have an issue with you. I personally believe that you cannot change them, though your reactions may keep the situation from getting worse. As I write this I've just intercepted a barrage of mean spirited texts from someone because we had a difference of opinion about the way something should be handled. Some people still show no other recourse than to resort to personal insults when they find themselves at odds over an issue. Whether it is a work, family or business related issue, it is cumbersome and flat out immature to deal in this manner; but sadly many do. In philosophy studies, we call this argumentum ad hominem. It is the act of attacking the person raising an argument instead of pursuing the merits or composition of the argument itself.

Yes, it can happen to the best of us and we all have room for growth, especially when rising tensions are a part of life. Take note, how you deal with difficult situations and difficult people will also shape your brand, so beware. This book is about re-valuing yourself and not allowing others to de-value you.

Another recent incident comes to mind. I worked on a production as an associate producer and copy writer for a corporate training video. I had a great relationship with my business partner, but he brought on a new person to direct and handle video production. Early on I could tell that he was dismissive or annoyed by any input that I had to offer. On the day of the shoot, while watching the video monitor, I noticed that the talent (which happened to be the COO of the company that hired us) was uncertain about where to look while the cameras were rolling. After a few minutes of filming, the director hadn't yet instructed the talent, so I leaned to ask him if the talent was certain of his eye line. With an air of consternation, the director snapped back with an admonishment to let him do his job. This was done in front of the client, which is breaking work etiquette rule number one. At that moment, I had to make a quick decision whether I was going to retort with the same snarl of a remark, which may have verbally vindicated me but which would not have reflected positively upon me for my associate, who owned the company that was hired to do the job. My associate did not speak up at that time. What do I do? In a flash it became clear. What may have been perceived as momentary embarrassment for me, would quickly fade if I did not respond in a like manner. I responded with a comment about team work, took a deep breath and remembered why I was there, which was to do a job and to do it well. Our director was there for his expertise in filming and coordinating the physical aspects of production, but I was also there as a producer to help oversee all aspects of production including representing the brand, the brand spokespersons on camera and any other aesthetics that are hard to describe but encompass an acute attention to detail for every frame that is captured on behalf of the company that hired us.

When I worked on national television campaigns for McDonalds, ReMax realty, Denny's and other major brands as a commercial spokesperson, I distinctly remember a director at the helm of the technical execution of the filming. Right behind him sat three or four executives from the advertising agency, and two or more people from the corporation whose product, message or service was being promoted. The director was indeed respected for his expertise, however, during the process, the agency and corporate heads intensely provided input and sometimes made slight modifications throughout the process. They functioned as a collaborative team with one goal in mind, to achieve the client's vision most authentically, to represent the brand and to make sure that there were no oversights because production time is costly. On that day, after the talent had left the room, and with the crew still present I went to the director and stated to him: "You don't have to like me, and we may never work together again, but you must respect me. I am a fellow producer on this, I was brought onto the project for a reason and that is to work as a team. My question to you was not intended to disrespect you. I am accustomed to working in environments where we leave our egos at the door and get the job done." He gave a half-hearted reply and asked that I just let him do his job.

That incident that day was probably one of the best things to ever happen to me! I was taken aback at the time and flustered that I even had to deal with such a mindset but as each moment unfolded, the true value of the experience was evolving. As I mentioned my mind was spinning with thoughts of how should I handle this.

#1 Though it was tempting, I decided NOT to let the foul attitude directed at me fester within me. I am not going to say that it was easy to resist, but I knew that I had a choice and I refused. That is NOT why I came to work that day. That day I DECIDED, notice that I did not say that I "felt." Feelings are generated by emotions; decisions are generated by the mind. I decided not to let the foul feeling fester.

#2 I decided to let the guy WITH the attitude HAVE the attitude. It was HIS CHIP on HIS SHOULDER and I wasn't bearing it. With each clear moment of thought, I felt myself getting stronger and stronger. In the past it would have deeply troubled me if someone did not like me or what I said or did.

#3 I decided to OWN that which I knew, and that which I was attempting to bring to the project. If I was attempting to bring VALUE but it was not welcomed, then it was STILL VALUABLE, whether that person recognized it or not. Remember, I said that every victory is not called right away. Just because someone does not see the value that you have or the value that you want to bring to the table, it does not mean that it is not valuable. It will only fail to be valuable to them, if they fail to recognize it for any reason.

#4 Stay the course as long as you are contracted to, then seek out other venues and/or associates with whom you have mutual respect. You may or may not win over a difficult person, but when and where YOU DO have CONTROL over your situation, take it! Fortunately for me I was an independent contractor on this and I did not have to contend with such an attitude on a regular basis.

#5 Decide to use the difficult person's attitude as an exercise. *Let their deficit in people skills, help strengthen a SURPLUS in your coping skills.* I did not say that this is easy, nor do I recommend submitting to long term malaise, but when you do have a choice or until you can seize the opportunity for a new work environment, business partner or customer, consider these aforementioned steps.

Realize that there are different types of leaders, those with clear and strong rules of respect and those where the lines are blurred. This is common with people pleasers and any number of people who don't want to be the bad guy or who are leery of confronting difficult situations where right, wrong, or clear codes of conduct have to be communicated or enforced. How someone else behaves can set you ajar when it is contrary to how you would behave in a situation. You may not always have a referee to call out foul play. How you handle these occurrences is as critical to your brand management as the brand itself.

As I drove home that evening, with one eye trained on the freeway and the other dialing my agent in Beverly Hills, I was insistent on returning to the leagues where I have worked and been paid as a union talent, where the pay scale is great and strong codes of ethics are enforced. Later that night I went to the International Movie Database and typed in my name. On the screen appeared over thirty credits in network television and motion pictures, not including television and radio commercials, or my seven years as a broadcaster for Armed Forces Radio and Television Services worldwide. I also saw a credit where I had been featured in a German TV documentary along with Bob Hope and Mickey Rooney. I was the only female and the only African American in such company. I looked up the director that I had worked with earlier that day and he had a much lesser amount of credits on the database. My comparison here is to illustrate the essence of a missed opportunity. On the low budget video that day I was willing to share experience that I had gained from having been on set with Steven Spielberg, Aaron Spelling, Oliver Stone, John Landis, noted commercial director Joe Pytka and on shows for NBC, ABC, CBS and more. It wasn't about hierarchy or my pay scale, I was a committed member of the team who was bringing my A game in the same manner that I would on any project, regardless of the pay.

When you are working with those who have a mindset of exclusion or a closed mindset, do not let it devalue your sense of worth, let the fault fall upon their failure to recognize. By the same token, don't let your years of expertise overshadow the talents of those who have fewer years than you, if there is something noteworthy in their skillset or if they have a new and valid approach to accomplishing a task.

I find this example worthwhile because if your focus is only on perfecting the product or service and making money, but not perfecting (or at least being open to improving) your personality or attitude about dealing with difficult people or situations, then your brand is still vulnerable. Working through these occurrences is akin to endurance testing the greatest resources in your business or organization, and that is Human Resources.

As for the urge or the natural impulse to defend, argue or put another person in check to counter your own embarrassment in a situation, take note that usually bad behavior repeats itself and soon enough the perpetrator will create his or her own reputation. Eventually it will precede them. However, you could permanently tarnish your reputation by giving a knee jerk reaction when someone else has acted out of character. When that happens, your company and your brand may suffer repercussions for the actions that you took in retaliation. Given today's instant climate of social media, you may encounter a mammoth amount of damage control. Sometimes when people, yes grown people, misbehave it's not an indication of how confident and self-assured they are, but how insecure and uncertain they are in their thinking, in their choice of actions and in their self-control.

This book is not about them, but about you who are cognizant enough to read it and consider how it can positively impact your life, who you are and what YOU present to the world. So let this be a warning, that you will encounter difficult people and difficult situations. Put these thoughts in your emergency response kit.

If you do have to work in a prolonged environment with a difficult person, just remember your values, refuse to stoop to a level that could backfire on you should the situation in question be illuminated. Take the high road, keep track of your written correspondence and don't put anything in writing anytime or anywhere that you would not want publicized. This includes all forms of electronic communications, especially emails and tweets. Your own good character is the best defense. Your refusal to respond in kind to negativity will send a message to the person that you only respond to respectful communication. You will build up a tolerance for resisting bad behavior, although you grossly detest it.

Sometimes you will encounter people who have pent up frustrations due to a work environment that you are not aware of. Perhaps you have been awarded a contract that they or one of their friends was vying for. Perhaps their CEO has insisted that they work with you, when they don't see a need for your position or line of services. Sometimes they will lash out at the closest point of contact, which could be you. You may even be stepping into a climate where empathy and mutual respect do not exist. These circumstances and situations are likely to occur.

I would wager to say that insecure people were that way long before they met you. Sometimes you become the object of their disdain and they just have not learned another way to communicate. Oh yeah, make sure that you have not been the perpetrator of this tension. If you have, and if you are bold enough to admit it, then face the person to whom you have been disagreeable and let them know that you have some things that you are working on within yourself that may have caused some dissention. Perhaps you're caring for an aging parent, you may have health issues, financial stress, a childhood complex or any number of things that may alter your mood. In many cases this will cause the other person to be more understanding towards you. Some will say 'that's your problem' and not waiver, but if you are making a consorted effort to be a better communicator and team player, then most people will meet you with the same regard. You may even win an ally in the end or maybe you agree to disagree but maintain a sense of mutual respect.

People are walking around with all kinds of problems and unresolved issues. Many of these people bring their problems to work and into their business dealings. Sometimes there is no way of knowing in advance and sometimes there are red flags all over. When you are in charge of hiring, accepting work or recruiting your own brand ambassadors, ask: Do you have any personal problems or prejudices working with men, women, people of a certain race, religion or personality type. Do you take suggestions well? Watch for body language. How do they refer to others? If they have nothing but insults for others, this is a sign of how they regard others. Speak up and dig for information.

In standing beside your brand, as your brand reach grows, you may or may not have the immediate luxury of hiring a large agency to hunt for personnel with extensive recruitment procedures. Your initial staff may come from family and friends, so adhere to these suggestions when adding the much needed help to your expanding empire. What took months or years for you to build could be blown by just one mishap from someone without people skills. On the other hand, extraordinary people skills can be a game changer when in close competition with a similar brand whose products are equivalent but whose customer service is poor.

Had I not learned to stand up for myself, I would not have written this book and you would not be reading this right now. So back to my story about the director who was, shall we say, unenthused about working with me. Guess what happened? Days later I declared victory! Days later after I had replayed the incident over and over in my head, I declared victory because I did NOT let it get the best of me, not then and not now. Days later I declared victory as I also replayed the countless harmonious and mutually respectful business dealings that I have had with colleagues over the past 30 years, this situation (although frustrating) was miniscule. MINISCULE!! Days later I realized that if, after even the best of all efforts, this person decided that he did not like me, did not agree with me and did not wish to work with me, I was still firm in my professional convictions, satisfied with my manner of service and still associated with a majority of associates with whom I had harmonious dealings. It was not a photo finish but a re-count that determined that this was indeed a victory after all.

In building muscles, strength and endurance training is a must! In life and in work environments it is unlikely that someone will throw 100lb metal weights at you, but their emotional baggage may come flying at you at any moment. I encourage you to build up emotional and psychological strength and endurance. It is a secret ingredient in building a strong brand.

Just like professional race drivers practice driving dangerous collision courses, you must also be able to anticipate and navigate sharp turns and obstacles so that they do not throw you off course. One false move can lead to the death of a valued relationship with a client or have a lethal impact on a business matter. You have to think fast and not over-react, for every action will come with its consequences. It's up to you whether those consequences are good or bad.

Being the Brand, that stands beside the Brand

I would like to thank my friend Pat Kirk, who encouraged me not to shy away from referencing my experience in TV and film, even in the business world. Pat is a former news reporter and anchor for several broadcast outlets including CNN and the Home Shopping Network. We met when she was the news director at a local radio station in Los Angeles, and I was on air as the morning drive side kick and Public Affairs Director. When the grind of news reporting and the frequent relocations that it required grew cumbersome for

Pat, she successfully landed at one high end corporate job after another, with stints at American Express, T Mobile and R. H. Donnelly. Pat insisted that there was a value that I could bring from the broadcasting and film industry that could be very beneficial in the work world. Pat was right. Our experiences shape our culture, what we bring to it and what we expect. The larger population may flock to movie theatres and praise the performance of a movie star, or director but what I witness on the set is that every moment of the day the entire team rallies in support of those few moments that happen in front of the camera. One team prepares the lighting, hanging huge fixtures, bracing reflectors on brackets, aiming gels and fabric covered frames ever so slightly to fit the Director of Photography's vision for how the scene should be lit. The audio department works to make sure that the actors are taped in with their respective mics, the boom man sometimes holds a large microphone in the air above his shoulder for hours, with a heavy power pack strapped around him, while another guy that the audience will never see sits monitoring the master sound track that is being recorded. Production assistants schedule all of the talent, cast and crew. They hang signs on landmarks for parking and easy directions to remote locations. May I mention that weather conditions may include extreme hot or extreme cold temperatures when these jobs are done. Meanwhile the camera crew is equally hard at work scurrying to make sure that various lenses are on hand, battery packs are charged, memory cards ample, cranes and dollies are nearby and at the immediate disposal of the director once he or she has given their direction for a particular shot. Also on hand are a number of men and women who work as grips and electricians. Theirs is a constant job of fetching, toting and plugging in any manner of camera equipment, cables and miscellaneous items that are needed. The transportation department is responsible for mobilizing the entire company, which includes huge trucks that store the cameras and production equipment, generators, mobile dressing rooms & lavatories, and even mini-vans for transporting the staff from designated parking areas to the set where we will be working. Notice, we haven't even gotten to the actors yet. The production department handles the administration of all this. On a daily basis any number of administrative logistics are handled by this department including securing locations, personnel, equipment, scheduling talent, processing call sheets, contracts and paperwork and everything else that happens to the actual film once it's in the can for the day. This department is also responsible for monitoring a detailed projection of what will be shot the following day and who will be needed. Hair and make-up departments are brought on to create the on camera look, while the wardrobe department may have started on the project weeks earlier. These departments may be headquartered elsewhere but when filming on locations, these departments set up mobile operations. Every facet of the team works to make those moments before the camera, authentic, memorable and in sync with the director's vision and hopefully within the budget that the producers have worked diligently to secure. My favorite department is Craft Services. They are the persons or the staff who has been hired to keep the crew well stocked with snacks throughout the day so that they have something to munch on between main meals. There are long hours on the set, with the crew often arriving several hours before the actors and performers. All it takes is for the director to change his or her mind about their vision for the shot that they would like to achieve and presto, the whole team is in action, just like that! The WHOLE TEAM moves instantly and in tandem to make movie magic occur. Think about that the next time you rush out of a movie theatre before the credits roll. These are not arbitrary names on a screen, these are real people who unselfishly give of themselves to make movie magic happen. Most of my experience has been on union sets where the performers belonged to the Screen Actors Guild, the American Federation of Television and Radio Artists (now merged as SAG-AFTRA) and the crew were members of the labor union called IATSE, the International Alliance of Theatrical Stage Employees. However, I have been on a few non-union sets. The level of expertise varies, but the overall sense of team work and sportsmanship is the same.

I now see how experiencing this type of team work has shaped my consciousness as a business person. I've also seen this type of teamwork in hospitals. Making movies is not a life or death situation, but just like in hospitals, the teams move and function on a moment's notice with all hands on deck and no time for egos or attitudes that do not move the whole team towards achieving a common goal. I would subconsciously have these expectations of people I met in the business world, and in the corporate world but that is indeed a different world. The difference is that for those in TV and film, for the most part, the people in this industry love what they do. They may or may not be well paid, but this is where they want to be and it drives them to be their best and give their all. You can feel it when you walk on almost any movie set.

So Pat Kirk was right. There is no need to downplay my experience in this arena. Television and film is big business worldwide. ABC, NBC and CBS are brands, and I stand beside these brands as companies whose productions I have worked on over the years. I have also worked on movie lots such as Paramount, Warner Bros, and Disney. I have learned from observing the eager production assistant who is the least paid on the set but hustles with urgency to meet the needs of his crew, without complaint or hesitation. I have also learned from the confident director who knows what she wants, but is also wise and humble enough to consult with her team to determine the best way to achieve her goal. I have observed people and processes. This shapes me and my personal brand, and adds to my expertise.

What about you? What experiences have you discounted that add greatly to your expertise? Experts are just people who have done something long enough that they have mastered it.

Experts have learned from their mistakes, faced their fears and now they show others how to do what it is that they have mastered. That's it! Barring any fancy terms, an expert is skilled at performing a task or applying a set of principles successfully. Their expertise is valuable because it provides a comfort level to those who are less confident in the same area of expertise.

During the evolution of my marketing and branding business, I realized that there were many millionaires who would seek my advice or they had agents or consultants who would do the same. One such associate is Jerrold Smith, the owner of 1 Plus One Management Inc., a company that has been involved in the marketing of Nix Check Cashing, which was at one time the largest check cashing chain in Southern California.

I had the great fortune of working at Jerrold's office at the time that Tom Nix, the founder of Nix Check Cashing, released his biography NIXLAND, My Wild Ride In The Inner City Check Cashing Industry. Tom trusted Jerrold implicitly and Jerrold trusted me. Together we came up with strategies to market his book. Though I had worked on various Nix Check Cashing radio spots over the last twenty years, it was a joy to be a part of this next juncture in Tom Nix's life.

Tom Nix's book revealed many enthralling facts about this powerful business man. He had worked in the family business while attending The University of Southern California (USC). As a kid he engaged in street fights, believed in fairness and often stood up for the little guy. Tom and his father started as a bakery distributor, then a convenience mart owner before starting Nix Check Cashing. Tom also worked as a sheriff in some of the most dangerous parts of Los Angeles. He did a lot for the community and grew the business to a chain of 60 outlets before selling it to Kinecta Federal Credit Union for $45 million in 2007.

Still with all of this success, I was touched by how transparent Tom Nix was about his personal life and how he decided to change:

"I took complete responsibility for everything in my life. I was no longer a victim.... I looked at life as a great adventure, good and bad. I looked for the silver lining in every situation. Experiences are our teacher."

(Nix, 2013, p. 81)

With Tom's track record & new desires as an author & speaker, we developed strategies to create Tom's digital imprint and to raise awareness of Tom's new book. We produced video vignettes where Tom told his story. We also heard from his colleagues and his wife. This gave him an enhanced presence online and one that now stood beside the brand for which he had become known.

I am proud to stand *beside* the Nix brand as a company who has trusted me to be the voice of the company on local radio commercials, and as a brand manager & consultant to a multi-millionaire turned author. I am proud to stand beside Jerrold Smith's 1 Plus One Management Incorporated as well as we continue to help businesses evolve.

Think back on your successes and failures. What have you learned that is of greatest value to your current or potential job or clients? Now consider what has been presented as far as branding? How many times have you stood behind a company or stepped aside and let someone else take total credit for work that you performed? When was it? Chances are it is a vivid memory.

List it here:_____

_____

With that now reflect on the questions in Step 2.

For those who still may be ambivalent about the brand beside the brand concept, here are some ways to reposition yourself.

Hi I am _____, an expert in the field of _____, I am (or we are) a brand that has been in proud association with (List the companies or projects here).

Through my efforts with these companies, we have successfully (List the achievements of the company or campaign. Feel free to boast of sales numbers, new business acquired, etc.).

These companies have trusted their business to me (or us). We proudly stand beside their brand, and consider it a great benefit to have the opportunity to stand beside your brand as well.

Next, in keeping with the suggestions of chapter eight, insist on your value right up front. Instead of offering up the whole store for free only to find out that your potential customer does not have a budget at all, consider this as an ice breaker in determining whether they are a viable lead for potential business.

I would be happy to consult with you. We have a range of products and services. The initial thirty-minute consultation is free, after that our fee for consultation is $_____ and that can be used towards goods and services, should you decide to do business with us. What is your budget range at this time?

Remember to ask the hard questions first. Although customers may contact you, they may not be ready to do business with you right now. You can save time on the front end by not over investing your time in a situation that has little or no potential for a revenue stream. Remember also that you can assist people in general during your volunteer time and community service. I believe in that greatly, but that is not what this book is all about. What you can do with clients who are tentative, is to help them gage their own readiness to do business. I have learned this by trial and error also. Once while doing marketing for a particular business, I had all of my stakeholders ready to launch a radio campaign for a grand opening, but the date kept changing. Because of my reputation with the station, I was able to negotiate perks and rearrange production schedules in order to meet the immediate demands of the client, only to find out that the client was not ready to open as soon as they thought that they were. There were scores of city approvals and licenses that were needed before the business could open. This was new territory so there were many questions that I did not know to ask in order to gage their actual readiness, as opposed to their desired readiness to open. The problem is that I put my radio associates in a frustrating position because I had such a solid reputation with them that when I said that a project was ready to go, it was indeed ready to GO! I greatly value the company that had contracted me and would spare no effort in satisfying their needs. However, as an independent business person myself, it is almost always a learning process. I have discovered that in protecting my brand, I must exhaust every effort to weed out potential problems or delays that a contract, client or project might have and work to solve potential problems before involving others who depend on me for solid business answers and not a waste of their time. Everything worked out in the end, after many false starts the business opened successfully. My reps at the radio station understood the nature of the business and did not hold me responsible for problems that arose due to the numerous changes of schedule.

At the end of the day, the difference is you. The world is populated with many amazing people who are pursuing similar callings in life. The difference is that people who come to you will do so because of something that you did, something that you said or something that someone else has said about you and the things that you do. In the business world we officially call this branding, marketing, advertising and promotions, but still it stems from you.

Warmly and firmly embracing a powerful message and then emitting that message into the world will prove to be the most sincere and forthright approach to presenting your newly evolved presence to the world.

No longer allow yourself to be intimidated to remain in the background when it comes to your work. You may not have an out front personality, and that is fine, but the products and services that you provide must be known, and you are the one to make them known by standing in your new position, *beside the brand.* You are the C. E. O. of Y-O-U, **your optimal universe.** Now go and be the brand that stands beside the brand always and forever more.

References

Ackerman Anderson, L. and Anderson, D. (2010) *Beyond change management: A change leader's roadmap.* Hoboken, NJ: Wiley and Sons pg. 53

Boothman, N. (2010) *How to convince them in 90 seconds or less.* New York, NY: Workman Publishing p. 269

Bureau of Labor Statistics Economic News Release, May 6, 2016 Table A-8 Retrieved from: http://www.bls.gov/news.release/empsit.nr0.htm

Hempel, J. (February 8, 2016) Wired.com. Retrieved from: http://www.wired.com/2016/02/twitter-is-now-worth-less-than-many-of-the-unicorns/

Johnson, Dr. S. (1998). *Who moved my cheese.* New York, NY: G. P. Putnam's Sons Publishing

Kondalkar, V. G. (2009) *Organization Development*, New Age International, pg. 29

Nadler, D. and Michael Tushman. Beyond the charismatic leader: Leadership and organizational change. *California Management Review* 32, no. 2 (winter 1990): ¶3 p77.

Nix, T. (2013) *Nixland: My wild ride in the inner city check cashing industry.* Irvine, CA: Business Ghosts Books p. 81

O'Reilly III, C.A. & Tushman, M.L. (1996) Ambidextrous Organizations: Managing Evolutionary and Revolutionary Change. *California Management Review, 38*(4): 8-30. DOI: 10.2307/41165852

O'Reilly III, C.A. & Tushman, M.L. (April 2004) Ambidextrous Organizations. Harvard Business Review. Retrieved from: https://hbr.org/2004/04/the-ambidextrous-organization

O'Reilly III, C.A. & Tushman, M. L. (2016) *Lead and disrupt,* Stanford University Press

Peck, M. Scott (1978) *The way of the road less travelled.* New York, NY: Simon & Schuster

More on LaRita Shelby and SB Music, Media & Marketing

Contractors and clients have included the Department of Defense, Southwest Tennessee College, The Women's Theatre Festival of Memphis, Olympian Kevin Young, Ascent Publishing, The Electronic Urban Report, Northrop Grumman, LMS Wings, Oscar Generale and more.

LaRita Shelby is available for speaking and workshops on the following:

- Being The Brand Beside The Brand
- Developing Finish Line Mentality
- Humorous Resources: HR's New Value in the Workplace
- Millennials & Baby Boomers: Customer Service & Generation Gaps

LaRita lives in Los Angeles with her son. She enjoys the balance of working in business, entertainment & the arts and education. Visit LaRitaShelby.com or email Bookme@LaRitaShelby.com.

www.ingramcontent.com/pod-product-compliance
Lightning Source LLC
Chambersburg PA
CBHW050555300426
44112CB00013B/1929